Food Groups

Grains

Lola Schaefer

Heinemann Library
Chicago, Illinois

© 2008 Heinemann Library
a division of Reed Elsevier Inc.
Chicago, Illinois

Customer Service 888-454-2279
Visit our website at www.heinemannraintree.com

Designed by Joanna Hinton-Malivoire
Printed and bound in China by South China Printing Co. Ltd.

12 11 10 09 08
10 9 8 7 6 5 4 3 2 1

ISBN-10: 1-4329-0141-9 (hc) -- ISBN-10: 1-4329-0148-6 (pb)

Library of Congress Cataloging-in-Publication Data
Schaefer, Lola M., 1950-
Grains / Lola M. Schaefer.
p. cm. -- (Food groups)
Includes bibliographical references and index.
ISBN 978-1-4329-0141-7 (hc) -- ISBN 978-1-4329-0148-6 (pb) 1. Grain in human nutrition--Juvenile literature.
2. Grain-- Juvenile literature. I. Title.
QP144.G73.S33 2008
613.2--dc22

2007008971

Acknowledgements
The publishers would like to thank the following for permission to reproduce photographs: © Corbis p. **7** (Dung Vo Trung); © Dreamstime.com p. **10** (barley, Ejla; corn, Dannyphoto80; oats, Emielcia; rice, Jameshearn; wheat, Kovalvs); © Harcourt Education Ltd pp. **4** (MM Studios), **11** (Tudor Photography), **15** (Tudor Photography), **16** (Tudor Photography), **18** (Tudor Photography), **19** (Tudor Photography), **20** (Tudor Photography), **22** (MM Studios), **26** (Tudor Photography); istockphoto.com pp. **14** (Michael Valdez), **25** (Kurt Holter); © Masterfile pp. **17**, **27** (Dan Lim); © Photodisc p. **9**; © Photolibrary pp. **6** (Anthony Blake), **8** (Anthony Blake), **12** (BananaStock) **13** (Anthony Blake), **21** (Foodpix), **23** (Foodpix), **24** (Stockbyte), **29** (Photononstop); © Punchstock p. **28** (BlueMoon Stock); USDA Center for Nutrition Policy and Promotion p. **5**.

Cover photograph reproduced with permission © Masterfile (G. Bliss).

Every effort has been made to contact copyright holders of any material reproduced in this book. Any omissions will be rectified in subsequent printings if notice is given to the publishers.

Contents

Some words are shown in bold, **like this**. You can find out what they mean by looking in the glossary.

What Are Grains?

Grains are the seeds of some plants. Wheat, rice, and corn are three different grains. People all over the world eat grains in bread, crackers, noodles, and pancakes.

There are many different kinds of foods made with grains.

Grains are one of the **food groups**. You need to eat grains each day as part of a good **diet**. Grains help your body stay healthy.

Where Grains Come From

Farmers plant seeds of grain in fields. The plants grow until they are **ripe**. Some farmers pick the ripe grains with large machines. Other farmers pick grains by hand.

Around the world, people eat more rice than any other grain.

This wheat flour will be sold in grocery stores.

The picked grains are taken to a place called a mill. Machines take the **kernels**, or seeds, from the plant. Some grain is ground to make **flour** or **meal**.

Making Grains into Food

Many foods can be made with **flours**. Bakers add water and other foods to flours. They make breads, cookies, cakes, or bagels.

A baker works with many different kinds of grains.

Onions and vegetables add flavor to rice.

Other grains, like oats and rice, are sometimes cooked in water or milk. The grains soften when cooked. People add **seasonings** to the grains and eat them.

How Grains Look

Many grains look alike. The **kernels** are smaller than the end of your fingernail. Each grain is longer than it is wide.

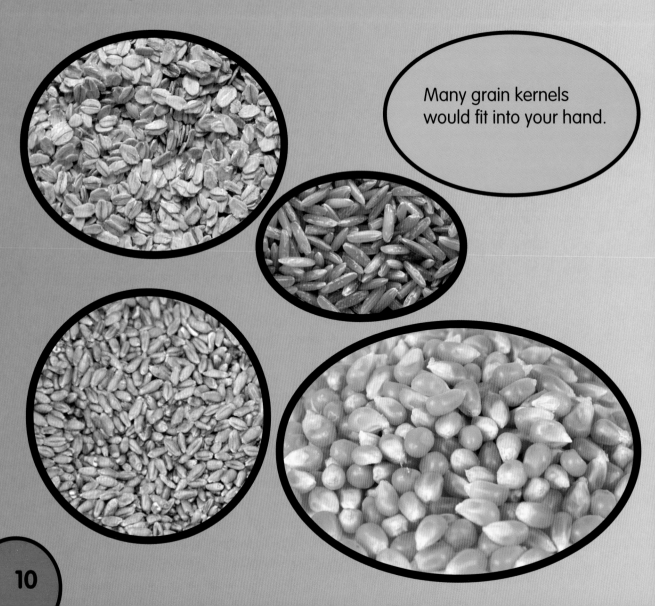

Many grain kernels would fit into your hand.

Corn kernels are small and almost round. They can be made into many things, such as these corn chips.

Most corn is yellow or white. Wheat is light brown. Rice can be black, brown, yellow, or white. Other grains are light brown or tan.

How Grains Taste

Many grains taste nutty. Some breads are made with the whole grain **kernel**. Those breads take longer to chew and have more flavor.

A ham sandwich made with whole grain bread is a healthy and tasty lunch.

Oatmeal is made from oats.

Most grains are cooked or baked before you eat them. Cooking makes the grains softer and easier to chew. Oats stay thick and chewy even after they have been cooked.

Why Grains Are Healthy

Grains are full of **vitamins**, **minerals**, and **carbohydrates**. Your body uses carbohydrates to make **energy** for work or play. Vitamins and minerals help keep your body healthy and strong.

The carbohydrates in pancakes help your body make energy.

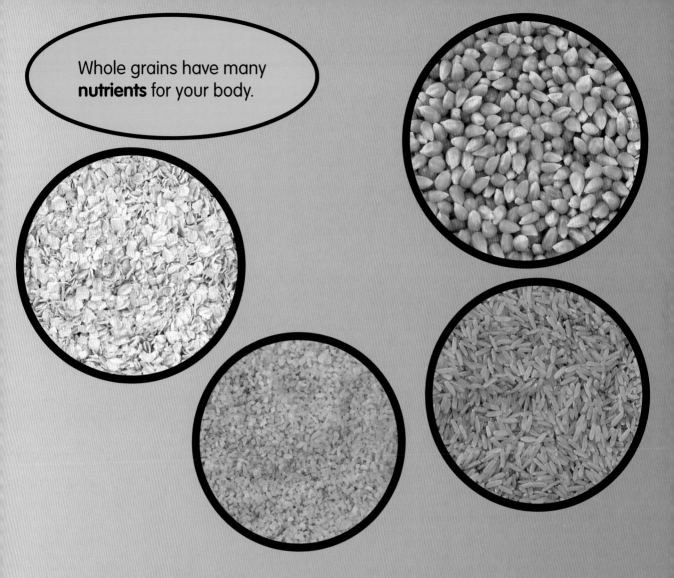

Whole grains have many **nutrients** for your body.

Whole grains that are made with the whole **kernel** are healthier. They have more carbohydrates and more **fiber**. Fiber helps your body use the vitamins and minerals it takes in.

How Many Grains Do You Need?

Most children 5–10 years old need 4–5 servings of grains each day. A serving could be a piece of toast or a portion of rice. It could be a bowl of pasta or a slice of pizza.

Each of these servings gives your body **nutrients** it needs.

Eat many different grains each day to stay healthy.

You should eat at least one serving of grains with each meal. Look for food labels that say "whole grain." These are the healthiest grains for your body.

Grains to Eat for Breakfast

Many breakfast foods are made with grains. A bowl of granola, oatmeal, or cornflakes makes a good breakfast. Pancakes, waffles, toast, and bagels are also made with grains.

Try eating a bagel with one of these different toppings for breakfast.

Crunchy bites

Please ask an adult to help you.

- Stir the oatmeal and powdered milk together.
- Add the rest of the ingredients and mix well.
- Roll into 1 in. (2.5 cm) balls and place in the refrigerator for 2 hours.
- Serve and enjoy.

You will need:
- ¾ cup of oatmeal
- ¾ cup of powdered milk
- ½ cup of crunchy peanut butter
- ½ cup of honey
- 1 teaspoon of vanilla
- ¼ cup of raisins

Eat three or four crunchy bites for a healthy breakfast.

Grains to Eat for Lunch

Many children eat sandwiches for lunch. Sandwiches are made with bread. Breads can be made with wheat, oatmeal, rye, or **spelt**.

Breads made with different grains have different flavors.

Tortillas can be made with a lot of different fillings.

Some children eat chips or crackers with their lunches. Others eat **tortillas**. All of these foods can be made with whole grains.

Grains to Eat for Dinner

Many people like to eat pasta for dinner. There are many different shapes of pasta to try. Maybe you like spaghetti, macaroni, or lasagna.

Whole grain pasta has a darker color and more flavor.

Couscous is made from ground wheat.

Couscous is another grain people eat for dinner. Sometimes people eat it with meat or vegetables, or they make a salad with it. Rice is also a very popular food for dinner.

Grains to Eat for Snacks

Popcorn is the whole **kernel** of corn heated until it bursts open. Breadsticks and sesame sticks are also crunchy snack foods. When you need a snack, try one of these.

Popcorn is a fun, healthy snack to eat.

Snap and crack snack

- Place the cereal and snacks in a bowl.
- Add the peanuts and walnuts.
- Mix everything together.
- Divide into sealed bags.
- Take a bag with you to enjoy a snack on the go.

You will need:
- 1 cup of a healthy cereal
- ½ cup of a snack such as small pretzels
- ½ cup of peanuts
- ½ cup of walnuts

This snack will give you **energy** and **fiber**.

Keeping Grains Fresh

Grains like rice, oats, wheat, or barley need to be stored in air-tight containers. They will keep well in a cool, dry space. They should be stored out of the sunlight.

It is good to store grains in plastic containers.

Wheat flour can be used to make bread soon after it has been bought.

Whole grains spoil quicker than other grains. Use these grains as soon as you can. Place them toward the front of your cupboard.

Do Grains Alone Keep You Healthy?

Grains are good for your body. But you need more than grains to stay healthy. Eat foods from each of the other **food groups** and drink plenty of water.

Foods from different food groups can be served together to make a good meal.

Your body rests and repairs itself while you sleep.

As well as eating healthy foods, your body needs regular **exercise**. You should try and get a little each day. You also need to get plenty of sleep each night. Sleep helps you stay strong and well.

Glossary

carbohydrate   part of food (such as bread or rice) that gives a person energy

diet   what a person usually eats and drinks

energy   power needed for a body to work and stay alive

exercise   physical activity that helps keep a body healthy and fit

fiber   rough part of food that is not digested. Fiber helps carry food through the body.

flour   grain, such as wheat, that is ground up and can be used for cooking or baking

food group   foods that have the same kind of nutrients. There are five main food groups, plus oils.

kernel   grain or seed of a type of plant

meal   ground grain that is larger than flour. People make foods with cornmeal.

mineral   nutrient needed to make the body work correctly

nutrient   substance (such as a vitamin, mineral, or protein) that the body needs to stay healthy and grow

ripe   fully grown and ready to pick or eat

seasoning   ingredient used to add flavor to food. Salt and pepper are two seasonings.

spelt   one of the first grains to be grown by early farmers. It has a nutty flavor, has more protein than wheat, and is high in fiber.

tortilla   flat, thin cake made from cornmeal or wheat flour

vitamin   nutrient in food that the body needs to stay healthy. Nutrients help the body work correctly.

Find Out More

Books to read

Alexander, Carol. *Grains*. New York: Scholastic, 2006.

Fowler, Allen. *The Wheat We Eat*. New York: Scholastic, 2006.

Leedy, Loreen. *The Edible Pyramid: Good Eating Every Day*. New York: Holiday House, 2007.

Miller, Edward. *The Monster Health Book: A Guide to Eating Healthy, Being Active & Feeling Great for Monsters & Kids*. New York: Holiday House, 2006.

Schuh, Mari. *The Grains Group*. Mankato, MN: Capstone Press, 2006.

Websites to visit

KidsHealth: The Food Guide Pyramid
http://www.kidshealth.org/kid/stay_healthy/food/pyramid.html

Nutrition Explorations
http://www.nutritionexplorations.org/kids/nutrition/pyramid-grain.asp

United States Department of Agriculture:
Inside the Pyramid - Grains
http://www.mypyramid.gov/pyramid/grains.html

Index